DATE DUE			

8011

690
BAR

Barber, Nicola.

Building for
tomorrow.

**MESA VERDE MIDDLE SCHOOL
POWAY UNIFIED SCHOOL DISTRICT**

FACING THE FUTURE

BUILDING FOR TOMORROW

FACING THE FUTURE

BUILDING FOR TOMORROW

Nicola Barber

RSVP
RAINTREE
STECK-VAUGHN
PUBLISHERS
The Steck-Vaughn Company

Austin, Texas

Library of Congress Cataloging-in-Publication Data

Barber, Nicola.
    Building for tomorrow / Nicola Barber.
        p.   cm.—(Facing the future)
    Includes index.
    Summary: Includes such topics as computer-aided design,
new methods of building, new ways to use glass, green buildings,
building for leisure and pleasure, floating worlds, and cities for
the next century.
    ISBN 0-8114-2805-2
    1. Building—Juvenile literature.   2. Building—Technological
innovations—Juvenile literature.   3. Buildings—Energy conservation—Juvenile literature.   [1. Building—Technological innovations.   2. Forecasting.]   I. Title.   II. Series.
TH149.B36   1993
690—dc20   92-24925
                                                       CIP
                                                        AC

Typeset by Tom Fenton Studio, Neptune, NJ
Printed in Hong Kong
Bound in the United States
1 2 3 4 5 6 7 8 9 0 HK 98 97 96 95 94 93

Acknowledgments

Editor – Su Swallow
Design – Neil Sayer

For their help and for information given, the author and publishers
wish to thank the following:
Dr. R. Skinner, Intermediate Technology; Sarah Conrado and
Fiona Millar, Sir Norman Foster and Partners; Simon Clay,
Kajima UK Engineering Ltd.; Fenella Gentleman and Hugh
Whitehead, YRM Parnership Ltd.; Taisei Europe Ltd.; Amanda
Levete, Future Systems; Wendy Dunning, CAD Consultant;
Pilkington plc; The Findhorn Foundation; Guilio Gallizzi, Crapnell
Chamberlain Associates; Peter Walker, Red Cross, Geneva;
Impact Structures Ltd.; Richard Rogers Partnership; Renzo Piano
Building Workshop Paris; (for information on the Kansai
International Airport Passenger Terminal Building on page 37)
Renzo Piano Building Workshop Paris (Renzo Piano and Noriak
Okabe), consultants Ove Arup & Partners International Ltd.;
Renzo Piano Building Workshop Japan k.k., Nilcken Sekkel Ltd.,
Aéroports de Paris, Japan Airport Consultants Inc.; Sir Norman
Foster and Partners for permission to include information about
the buildings on page 6 (Toulouse), page 9 (Hong Kong and
Shanghai Bank), page 12 (Museum of Prehistoric Mankind),
page 17 (Duisbury), page 39 (Commerzbank), page 40 (Berlin
masterplan), page 42 (Millenium Tower). The quotation on
page 22 is courtesy of the NMB Bank. The illustration on page
37, by Jon Swallow, is based on reference material kindly
supplied by Kajima Corporation, Tokyo, Japan.

For permission to reproduce copyright information the author
and publishers gratefully acknowledge the following:

Cover photographs – page 19 – Robert Harding Picture Library.

Title page – Hong Kong – Jones/ECOSCENE.
Page 4 – (top) Pilkington plc – (bottom) Nigel Smith, Hutchinson
Library; page 5 – Gerald Cubitt, Bruce Coleman Limited; page6
– Richard Davies, Sir Norman Foster and Partners; page 7 – (all)
produced for Holmes Associates for Channel 4 *Signals* by CAL
Videographics and YRM Partnership Ltd.; page 8 – R.B. Adda
Systems; page 9 – Ian Lambot, Sir Norman Foster and Partners;
page 10 – Richard Rogers Partnership, Otto Baite, P.A.
Technology, Princeton; page 11 – (top) Val and Alan Wilkinson,
Hutchison Library – (bottom) B. Regent, Hutchison Library;
page 12 – Sir Norman Foster and Partners; page 13 – (top)
Robert Harding Picture Library – (bottom) Renzo Piano Building
Workshop Japan; page 14 – Winifried Wisniewski, Frank Lane
Picture Agency; page 15 – Neyla Freeman, Bruce Coleman
Limited; page 16 – (left and right) Pilkington plc; page 17 –
(left) Richard Davies, Sir Norman Foster and Partners – (right)
Scandinavian Airline Systems; page 18 – Michael Macintyre,
Hutchison Library; page 19 – Robert Harding Picture Library;
page 20 – (top) Professor Gustav Peichl – (bottom) Richard
Davies, Future Systems; page 21 – Gryniewicz/ECOSCENE;
page 22 – Bob Fluemer aerial photography b.v., NMB Postbank
Groep; page 23 – (both) Sally Morgan/ECOSCENE; PAGE 24 –
(main) Robert Harding Picture Library – (inset) Sarah Errington,
Hutchison Library; page 25 – (top) Roland Sewell, Oxfam –
(bottom left) Richard Stanley, Oxfam – (bottom right) Chris
Dammers, Oxfam; page 26 – Alsop & Störmer; page 27 – (top)
Impact Structures Ltd. – (bottom) Richard Horden Associates
Ltd.; page 28 – Michael Macintyre, Hutchison Library; page 29
– (both) Intermediate Technology; page 30 – Intermediate
Technology; page 31 – (all) Neil Cooper, Intermediate
Technology; page 32 – Robert Harding Picture Library; page 33
– Jeremy Hartley, Oxfam; page 34 – (top) Michael Freeman,
Bruce Coleman Limited – (bottom) Spectrum Communications;
page 35 – (top) Helmut Fischer GmbH – (bottom) Expo 92;
page 36 – Robert Harding Picture Library; page 37 – Masahiko
Tanaka; page 38 – Neil Duncan, Brian Clouston and Partners,
Hong Kong; page 39 – (left) Sir Norman Foster and Partners –
(right) Richard Davies, Sir Norman Foster and Partners; page 40
– Sir Norman Foster and Partners; page 41 – D. & J. McClurg,
Bruce Coleman Limited; page 42 – (both) Richard Davies, Sir
Norman Foster and Partners; page 43 – Peter Menzel, Science
Photo Library.

Contents

Introduction

How often do you stop and think about the building that you are in? Is it a pleasant place or somewhere you are glad to get out of? How old is it, and how long do you think it will last? For many people, buildings are simply the places where they live, work, or spend their leisure time. Most of us do not give much thought to the design of a building. Sometimes a new building will arouse interest because it looks unusual. But for most people in the **developed world,** the layout of a building is something that is usually left to a specially-trained person, the architect, and only rarely do the people who will eventually live in a house or work in an office become involved in the design and building processes.

In the countries of the **developing world** the situation can be rather different. The majority of people build their own houses, often using skills and designs that have been passed down for generations. The variety of buildings constructed across the world is huge, depending on the climate of the region, the materials available, and many other factors. Some people are so poor that they cannot afford to build any kind of shelter at all. It is estimated that over half a million people live on the streets of Calcutta in India, forced to exist on pavements.

Building for Tomorrow looks at buildings and the people who design and build them, in both the developed and developing world. It describes some of the projects that are helping people to build more effectively for themselves, and looks at new methods of building that are being exploited in the developed world. Some new methods rely on techniques that have been used for centuries by traditional builders, while others depend on the latest technology, using the most up-to-date materials in new and sometimes daring ways.

One issue that seems likely to become more and more important as the twenty-first century progresses is that of **energy conservation** and renewal. **Fossil fuels** such as coal, oil, and gas are taken from the rocks in the Earth's crust, and will one day run out or become too difficult and expensive to extract. Renewable sources of energy, such as wind and solar power, not only

Modern buildings (above) in the industrialized countries of the developed world contrast sharply with slum dwellings found in many cities in the developing world (below, Manaus in Brazil).

4

Traditional village houses in Sulawesi, Indonesia, have bamboo roofs, although corrugated iron is being used more and more as it lasts longer than the bamboo. The sweeping roof shape may be to protect the houses against the heavy monsoon rains, or it may copy the shape of a buffalo horn, as buffalos are a sign of wealth to the local people.

provide power without pollution, but they will also never be exhausted. Buildings use up vast amounts of energy in their manufacture, construction, and maintenance. Many people are now becoming more aware of the need to conserve energy at all these stages, and examples of "green," or environmentally sound, buildings can be found in many countries.

Many of the plans for buildings of the future many never get further than the drawing board, but they provide clues to the way that tomorrow's architects will be thinking. Some of the most spectacular ideas are for super-high-rise skyscrapers, twice as high as the Sears Tower in Chicago which is the present record holder at 1,454 feet, underground cities, and even huge floating structures built out on the ocean. And when there is no more room for the Earth's rapidly increasing population, where will people go? Into space, to the colonies that may be established on Mars one day in the future.

You have a chance to discuss some of the issues examined in **Building for Tomorrow** by considering the questions in the **Looking at buildings** boxes. Words in bold type in the text are explained at the end of each section.

developed world – a term used to describe the rich, industrialized countries of Europe, North America, Japan, and Australasia.
developing world – a term used to describe the poorer countries of Africa, Asia, and Latin America. Many of these countries have economies that rely largely on agriculture.
energy conservation – the principle of using as little energy as possible to make something work.
fossil fuels – coal, oil, and natural gas. They are formed out of animal and plant remains trapped in rocks.

Computer-Aided Design

Designers have to be able to put their ideas down on paper, whether they are designing a piece of furniture, a toy, or a building. Presenting ideas on paper allows clients to change or approve the design, and manufacturers to work out the best way of making the product. Until recently all architects designed buildings on paper. Today, however, many architects use computers to speed up the process. They use a system called computer-aided design (CAD). One of the main advantages of CAD is that once a drawing has been fed into the system it can easily be changed and adapted. There is no need for time-consuming and costly redrawing; by feeding in the correct commands to the computer an image can be enlarged or reduced and changes can be made, so the architect can experiment with different solutions to a particular problem.

Some large, multistory structures, such as hospitals and office buildings, may have certain features that are repeated many times. CAD can duplicate these elements — elevators, staircases, and toilets for example — and arrange them on each floor of the building in seconds. If changes need to be made, the computer can copy them on to each floor plan very quickly. An architect drawing by hand would have to alter each floor plan separately.

Layering

When an architect is drawing by hand, he or she produces "working drawings" to show how the building will be constructed. The information is divided into layers: one layer might show the walls, windows, and doors, another might show the plumbing and drainage details, and another the furniture plan. Different sets of information can be mixed as necessary. The same effect can be achieved electronically with CAD. Some CAD machines have up to 256 layers that can be used, each representing a different set of information. The layers can be seen on the computer screen in different colors.

When the layers are printed out separately, they provide the information needed by the various manufacturers who will supply parts for the building. The layer showing the structural steelwork, for example, can be sent to the steel manufacturer, complete with all the **specifications.** The ground-plan can be sent to the **contractors** working on the site, so that they can lay the foundations for the building.

In the future this technology will be taken one step further. Data about the size and shape of the parts of a building will be sent directly to the manufacturers from the CAD system. The information from the computer will be used to drive the machines that cut out the parts for the building. This system will probably be used particularly for **prefabricated buildings.** It is already in use in other areas of industry, such as shipbuilding and car manufacture.

Λ guided tour

Computers can go one step further than any hand-drawn plans. CAD allows the architect and client to "walk" through a building, even before a brick has been laid on site. It is now possible to produce three-dimensional

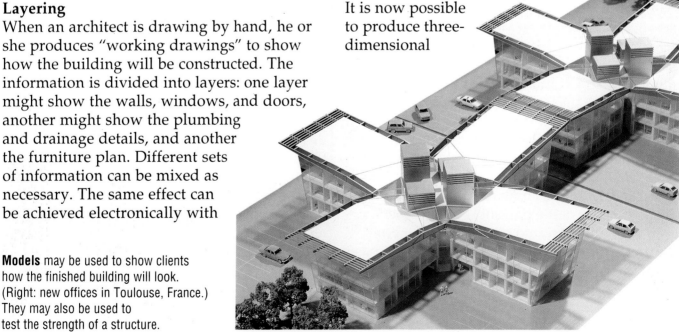

Models may be used to show clients how the finished building will look. (Right: new offices in Toulouse, France.) They may also be used to test the strength of a structure.

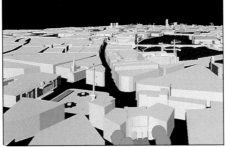

images of a building on the screen. These images can be moved around on the screen to allow the architect or client to look at them from any angle.

The next step will be to create a completely artificial world by using a virtual reality system. A client would put on a headset to experience what it would be like actually to stand inside and walk through the building that is being designed. Information about the building would be projected from a computer on to a screen inside the headset in front of the client's eyes. A movement of the head triggers the computer which changes the picture on the screen, allowing the client to explore the building without taking a step!

A CAD view of the capital.
These 3D pictures of development in London show existing structures in white, new buildings in blue, new sites in green, and proposed projects in red, orange, and yellow.

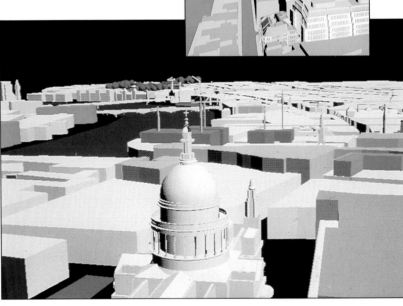

Flying over London

Some architects have already programmed the layout of whole cities into their computers. So now it is possible to "fly over" a city such as New York or London on a computer screen, moving or hovering over certain sites as necessary. This allows the architect to see how a new building will fit in with existing structures, and how it will affect a city's skyline. The architects from the firm called YRM put together a CAD sequence of images that took the viewer on a flight over London, highlighting the new developments in the city. The sequence contains 1,500 frames, and took about two months to create. Left to run at normal speed it lasts for just one minute, but the sequence can be stopped at any time to check a particular detail.

specifications – detailed descriptions and measurements.
contractors – the manufacturers and builders who supply the materials and labor needed to construct a building.
prefabricated buildings – buildings made up of parts that are made beforehand and delivered to the site ready to go in position.

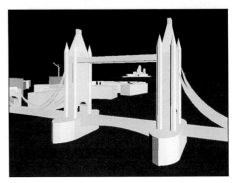

New Methods of Building

In the countries of the developing world most people have to rely on local materials — for example wood, stone, and mud — and follow traditional designs for their buildings, using simple techniques tested over hundreds of years. However, in the developed world, materials can usually be transported easily from one place to another, and most buildings are designed and built not by the people who will live and work in them but by trained architects and engineers. New designs have led to the invention of completely new methods of building, and new ways of using materials. Perhaps the most important research is that which is now looking into ways of conserving energy in buildings. New building methods keep costs down and provide more flexible buildings.

In some buildings the most up-to-date technology and materials are being used to construct the offices and houses for tomorrow. But in other cases architects are returning to traditional methods and materials in their designs for the twenty-first century.

Cheaper buildings

One way to make buildings easier and cheaper to construct is to prefabricate parts of a building on a large scale. Windows, doors, wall panels, and even floors and ceilings are made to standard sizes and shapes in factories. These mass-produced parts can be chosen by an architect from a catalog. They are then built into houses, shops, factories, and many other buildings that may be individually designed, and may look very different from one another in spite of the standard elements.

It is not only small parts of buildings that can be supplied by mass production. Whole rooms can be designed and mass-produced to meet the needs of a particular client and put together to make a complete building. They are manufactured in sections in a factory. One 82-bedroom hotel took only 34 weeks to build in this way. A similar hotel built by the traditional method could take up to five times as long to finish. Each room, known as a "module," in this hotel was made up of a steel box, wrapped in **insulation** and fireproof board, then sealed with a waterproof covering. Inside, the module was completely furnished with carpets, curtains, shower and toilet, lights, and even furniture before it left the factory. The modules were transported to the site by truck and positioned in a steel framework. Then the modules were covered with conventional roofing and wall materials, such as tiles and brick. This method of construction is often used for small buildings.

Prefabricated method. A hotel room is put together at the factory, complete with furnishings.

The room is wrapped in insulation and sealed in a waterproof covering before being taken to the site.

The modules are fitted together to make up the hotel.

High tech in Hong Kong. The headquarters of the Hong Kong and Shanghai Bank (right) rise above the older office blocks. Inside, the atrium (below) links offices on different floors and provides plenty of natural light.

High-tech solutions

A new style of architecture which has developed in the last 20 years is known as "high tech." In high-tech buildings the framework that holds the building up, and the **services** that keep the building running, are not hidden behind walls or above ceilings, but are put on display, as a design feature of the building.

The Hong Kong and Shanghai Bank headquarters in Hong Kong, designed by Sir Norman Foster, is a recent example of high-tech architecture. The skeleton of the 47-story building can be seen clearly from the outside. Inside, the floors are hung from the frame, like a road from a suspension bridge. The frame, in turn, is supported by eight massive masts. This design produces a huge open space, called an **atrium**, in the center of the building. The atrium space is used as a banking hall on the first floor and provides light for the upper floors. All the services for the building, such as electricity cables, heating and **air-conditioning ducts**, and elevators are on the east and west sides of the building, leaving more useful open space inside. Another high-tech building with an "inside out" construction is the Lloyd's Building in London, designed by Richard Rogers. Air-conditioning ducts, elevators, and toilets are located in six towers that run up the outside of the building. This allows the large floors inside to be left uncluttered, so the people who work in the building can divide up the floor space with partitions in the way that suits them best, changing the layout of their office space as necessary.

In the future more buildings are likely to be built that are easily adapted by the people that live and work in them. These buildings will

The Patscenter in Princeton, New Jersey. The services are suspended above the building.

grow and change as people's needs change. Some high-tech buildings already come very near to this ideal of a completely flexible building. Near Princeton University a building with offices and laboratories called the Patscenter was built for a company called PA Technology. The company wanted a building that could be adapted to suit different research projects. It was also important that the building could be extended. Richard Rogers designed a building made up of nine modules, each held up by a steel frame. If necessary, more modules can be added to the original nine.

Going underground

High-tech architecture is designed to provide flexible working spaces and buildings that are easy to maintain. The end results are often unusual and flamboyant buildings which stand out from their surroundings and which have often caused a good deal of discussion and controversy. But instead of building upward, some architects are more interested in the possibilities of using space under the ground for offices, houses, recreation centers, swimming pools, factories, and even power stations.

Throughout history people have dug underground shelters to live in. In a remote part of northwestern Scotland are found the remains of sunken Bronze Age halls, called "soddies." In the Matmata mountains of northern Africa, on the edges of the Sahara Desert, the Berber

people have, for 400 years, dug deep into the soft rock to create two- or three-story underground houses. In a remote mining area of South Australia, which supplies almost 90 percent of the world's opals, some of the miners and their families live in underground caves furnished with every modern convenience.

People have often built underground shelters because no building materials were available for building above ground. But underground houses solve another problem, that of temperature in extreme climates. The earth does not transfer heat easily, so during the day heat from outside moves only slowly to the inside of the house, and the house remains cool compared to the temperature outside. At night, when the temperature outside is lower, heat is retained inside the house, and the house stays comparatively warm. In Norway it has been found that 70 percent less energy is used to heat swimming pools built underground compared with conventional pools above ground, because the temperature below ground remains more stable.

In the United States, at least 5,000 American families live in underground houses, particularly in the central states where the summers are very hot, the winters very cold, and tornadoes are a threat. At the University of Minnesota one of the buildings on the campus extends 26 feet below ground level. Natural light is provided by windows that open on to a sunken triangular-shaped courtyard in the center of the building. Window boxes underneath each layer of windows are planted with vines. In summer the vine leaves prevent too much sunlight from entering the building. In winter the vines lose their leaves so as much light as possible enters the building. In another underground building on the campus a more sophisticated method is used to light the interior. The world's largest periscope channels light from the street above down into the building. Despite huge temperature changes from winter to summer, the temperature inside both buildings is maintained at a constant level, thanks to the insulating properties of the earth around them.

Another advantage of building underground is that the land above the building can be used for some other purpose; it is not lost once the building has been constructed. This is an important factor in countries such as Great Britain and Japan, which have dense populations and only limited space. Underground buildings can, for example, help to preserve what is left of the undeveloped countryside. This is what happened in the Snowdonia National Park in Wales, where the construction of a huge hydroelectric power station in an area of such outstanding natural beauty would have caused a public outcry. Instead, the power station was built in 10 miles of tunnels deep inside the Elidir Mountain, leaving the surface almost completely untouched.

Five underground dwellings have been combined to make a hotel (below) in Matmata, Tunisia (main picture). Circular holes in the ground show where houses have been built underground.

Often space does not have to be dug out in order to build underground. Instead, old mine shafts can be used. In many European countries underground caverns are used as storage space for drinking water, oil, or gas. In the United States old mine shafts have also been adapted for offices, industry, and warehouses.

Sometimes building underground is the most appropriate method of building for a particular landscape. The architects of the new Museum of Prehistoric Mankind, to be built in Verdon, France, have sited the building carefully in order not to spoil the beauty of the area. The region is one of ravines and gorges, famous for its caves and prehistoric settlements. The new museum is cut into the hillside so that the two-story building appears to be almost completely buried. Inside, light floods into the main hall and offices through a partly-glazed roof. The exhibition rooms underneath the offices are lit by artificial light.

Designing for climate

People all around the world have developed their own methods of building which reflect the climate in which they live. In hot, dry regions such as the Middle East, buildings have thick walls of stone or mud so that heat is only slowly transferred to the inside. The roofs of the buildings are flat, or shallow domes, in order to expose as little area as possible to the fierce sun. Houses are built close to each other around courtyards, which are cooled by the shadows they cast. People in hot, wet climates, in Indonesia and Malaysia for example, often build their houses on stilts to get extra ventilation. The roofs are steep and overhang the walls, to give good protection against rain.

The most famous example of traditional housing in extremely cold areas, the igloo, is now no longer commonly used. Igloos were constructed by the Inuit people in the Arctic regions using the only available resource — snow. Inside an igloo it was possible to maintain a comfortable living temperature using only the heat from blubber oil lamps and peoples' bodies, while the temperature outside could be as low as -40°F.

Many of these buildings may seem primitive when compared with modern ones. But traditional building methods often present the simplest and most effective solutions to the problems of sun , rain, wind, or snow. Too often, modern buildings work against nature rather than with it, relying on technology to control the extremes of climate. Air-conditioning keeps houses and offices in many countries at the same temperature, no matter what the weather is like outside. Central heating pumps out heat during the cooler months of the year. The problem with these modern solutions is that they are very costly to run, and they use up vast amounts of energy. Most of this energy is generated by burning fossil fuels such as coal and oil, resources that one day will run out, or become too difficult and expensive to extract. It is vital that world energy consumption is reduced. Architects across the world should look once again at the methods of

The new Museum of Prehistoric Mankind, in southern France, will be set in the hillside. The mast will be 197 feet high, with a viewing platform 49 feet up and video cameras at the top to give views of the surrounding countryside.

traditional builders in order to design buildings that will work with the climate, and not against it. (See the chapter, "Green Buildings," for more about ways of conserving energy.)

A new building being constructed on the Pacific island of New Caledonia will be kept cool without using an air-conditioning system. Here, Renzo Piano has produced an unusual design for a center to celebrate the culture of the local Kanak people. The building lies on a spit of land between the ocean and a lagoon, and is topped by clusters of tall, shell-like shapes built out of ribs of pine covered with bamboo and bark. These "shells" create a natural ventilation system, directing cool air down into the building, while warm air rises up and out through ventilation slats. A constant flow of cool air is forced through the building.

In cold climates the priorities are rather different. In Norway two architects, Eilif Bjørge and Anne Brit Børve, used an electric fan, piles of fine wheat particles, and a scale model to copy the effects produced by high winds and drifting snow. They were responsible for the

The tall shell shapes on top of the new cultural center in New Caledonia are designed to cast shade and to direct cooling winds down into the building.

design of a group of houses in the world's northernmost city, Hammerfest. It is winter for about eight months of every year in Hammerfest, and heavy snow often traps people in their houses for days on end. If the houses face the wrong way, windows and doors can become completely blocked. The new houses face south so that they make the most of the sun's light and warmth. They were shaped to make sure that the front of each was kept clear of snow, and the drifts accumulated at the back. Here, the architects were able to update and improve the traditional building methods.

Using natural materials

Buildings that are designed with climate and energy conservation in mind often make use of natural materials such as earth and timber. Underground houses (see page 10) and earth-built houses both exploit the fact that heat does not travel through earth easily. In the U.S., many new earthen houses have been built in the hot southern states such as New Mexico and Arizona. These buildings are called adobe houses, from an Arabic word *atobe* meaning a sun-dried brick. In Scandinavia, the roofs of timber houses are often covered with a thick layer of earth and turf. This provides an extra layer of insulation, preventing heat from escaping. This idea has been taken up by builders in other countries. It is now possible to buy waterproof roofing materials that allow you to plant a garden on top of your house, and save energy at the same time.

Lumber is one of the oldest building materials. However, tree planting worldwide has never kept pace with tree cutting and many forests are now vanishing alarmingly quickly. Some of the most vulnerable areas of forest are found in the rain forest of South America, Africa, and Asia. Much of the rain forest in

Turf on the roof helps to insulate wooden houses in cold climates (below, in Sweden).

these regions has been destroyed to provide more land for ranchers and for mining companies, and to provide tropical hardwoods for building and other uses. In Europe, 80 percent of all exterior woodwork, such as doors and window frames, is made of tropical hardwoods. Hardwood, as its name suggests, is harder and longer-lasting than softwood. However, softwood trees grow faster than hardwoods, and treatments are now being developed that can make softwood almost as durable as hardwood.

Lumber is a healthy building material because, like brick and stone, it is porous. This means that it breathes, allowing air and moisture through. This natural ventilation process is one of the main features of the environment-friendly houses built by members of the Findhorn Community in Scotland. The lumber used to build their houses is mostly taken from local softwood forests, but some houses are built out of old wood vats, once used to make whiskey! The outside walls are made up of a double layer of lumber. The space in between is filled with a layer of cellulose material made from recycled paper. This insulates the house and prevents heat loss — essential in the climate of northeastern Scotland.

Adobe houses in New Mexico. The windows are very small, to help keep out the heat of the sun.

Looking at buildings
● If you were asked to design a home for your family or friends, what materials and building method would you use and why?

insulation – materials that do not allow heat or cold (or sound or electricity) to pass through easily.
services – all the supplies that are needed to maintain and run a building, such as electricity, gas, water, heating, elevators, and so on.
atrium – a large open space, often extending several floors in the middle of a building, with a glass roof to allow light to enter.
air-conditioning/heating – a system of keeping the inside of a building at a constant temperature by cooling or heating air as it enters the building.
duct – a tube or pipe used to carry the services of a building.

New Ways with Glass

Some building materials are thousands of years old, but, with the help of modern technology, they are now being used in new forms and new ways. Glass is one of the most spectacular examples of an old material being transformed. Glassmaking dates back to about 4000 B.C. when people in the Near East first learned how to melt sand and wood ash together to make glass beads. The Romans perfected the art, and invented the method of blowing glass to make hollow shapes. Today, more than 90 percent of the flat glass produced in the developed world is made by a method called the float glass process (see below).

Glass can now be used to make whole walls of a building — not just the windows. The first buildings with glass "curtain walls" had metal frames to hold the glass in place. Today, sheets of glass can be sealed with a clear joint so that the curtain wall appears to be one huge sheet of glass. Modern glass can be tinted different colors, or mirrored so that it reflects the scene on the outside but does not allow people to see in. Coatings on glass can also prevent too much heat from entering the building by reflecting the sun's heat while still allowing light through.

Glass can also be used to save energy inside a building. Double or triple layers of glass in a window help to stop heat from escaping. Glass with a clear, low-emissivity coating will also help. This type of glass lets in light and heat from the Sun as well as reflecting heat from inside back into the building. This can improve the insulation of a room by up to 50 percent and cuts down on the energy needed to heat a building. Another method, which has been successfully used in the Ulm Institute for Accident Research in Germany, is to use glass panels containing **holograms**. The holograms can be controlled to change the amount of light entering the atrium area of the building. They can also be used to focus the light on to solar panels (see page 21) that lie beneath, in order to increase the energy produced.

One common use of glass in recent years,

Glass curtain walls (above) are often designed to reflect the surroundings rather than allow passersby to see in. (Left) Flat glass that has been made by the float glass process is moved on rollers.

A **model** (left) of the glass business center to be built in Duisburg, Germany and (below) one end of the huge atrium that lights the SAS airline building in Stockholm, Sweden.

apart from windows and curtain walls, has been to glaze the roofs of atriums. A spectacular atrium can be found in the Scandinavian Airlines building in Stockholm. The glazed area extends along the middle of the huge building, linking all the offices. It contains eating places, trees, and waterfalls and is used as a meeting place for employees. It helps to save energy by using solar energy to warm the building, and by cutting down on the amount of artificial light needed in the offices.

Glass will be used for a project called the International Forum for Tokyo. This building is to be a center for conferences, exhibitions, concerts, and theatrical performances. Its heart will be the Glass Hall, a huge building, shaped like an ellipse, 190 feet high. It will be covered by a vast glass roof, the largest in Tokyo. Another elliptical glass building is to be constructed in Duisburg, Germany. This is the new Business Promotion Center, designed by Norman Foster. It will be used for exhibitions and provides office space for small businesses. The building will have three "skins": an outer layer of glass, a middle layer of blinds (controlled by computer), and an inner layer of insulation material to prevent the building from becoming too hot or too cold. It will provide a new landmark for the people of Duisburg.

Looking at buildings
● Next time you visit a large town or city, see how many different types and uses of glass you can spot.

hologram – a three-dimensional image formed by using light from a laser.

Green Buildings

The greenhouse effect is a problem that must be tackled by the countries of the developed world because, although they contain only one-quarter of the world's population, they use three-quarters of the world's energy. Designing buildings that will conserve energy is becoming increasingly important. In the industrialized world, about half the greenhouse gases that contribute to the greenhouse effect are related to buildings — their manufacture, maintenance, and use. To design buildings with energy conservation in mind, the architect must consider the site, the local climate, and how the building will be ventilated, heated, and lighted. Architects of green buildings also need to take into account the wishes of the people who will eventually use the building, and what will happen to the building materials once the building comes to the end of its life. If all these factors are taken into consideration, then the buildings of the future will no longer contribute to the poisoning of our planet, and they will be healthier places to live and work.

Sick buildings

People in the developed world may spend up to 90 percent of their time indoors, in houses, offices, shops, schools, and factories. Until recently, little attention was paid to how healthy these indoor environments were. But it is now acknowledged that the air inside buildings is often more polluted than the air outside. Since the 1980s, more and more people have complained of a long list of minor illnesses which occur at work and disappear when they go home. Coughs, colds, headaches, skin allergies, and eye irritations are just some of the symptoms that people suffer. This problem is called "sick building syndrome," and it is now recognized as an official illness by the World Health Organization.

Researchers have discovered that sick building syndrome is most common in modern offices with air-conditioning systems. The air that is pumped through a system can sometimes be contaminated with microbes and fungi. People inside an air-conditioned building have no control over their environment — they cannot open a window or control the temperature of their surroundings. This is a factor thought to cause stress and illness. The flickering of artificial lighting and the glare from computer screens can cause headaches. Even the building materials and furnishings can

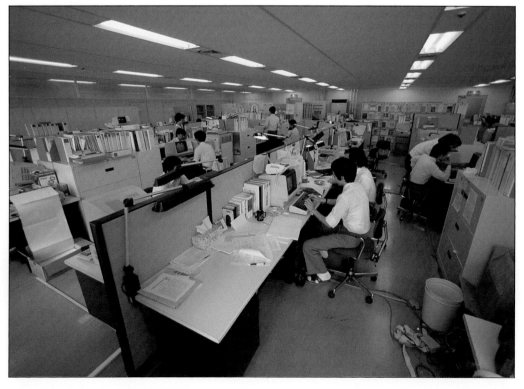

Many modern offices have little natural light or fresh air, depending instead on artificial lighting and air-conditioning, which can make some people feel ill.

The green office. Architects and engineers worked together to produce this design for an energy-efficient office building that has plenty of natural light and ventilation. Air is drawn into the buildings at the bottom and leaves through louvers at the top. The whole structure stands on a steel tripod, leaving space for a park for employees at ground level.

cause problems. The boards often used in the walls and ceilings of modern buildings can give off a gas called formaldehyde, which has been linked with skin and eye irritations. Some furnishings release other **toxic** vapors.

Saving energy

Some countries are far more advanced than others in their approach to green design and to energy conservation in particular. The Scandinavian countries have had energy-saving policies for many years. In the German-speaking countries many architects follow the principles of *baubiologie* or building biology, an approach that aims to design healthy, low-energy buildings, which have as little impact on the environment as possible.

Energy conservation can be achieved at all stages of a building's life — design, construc-

tion, and maintenance. Even the materials from which a building is made can have an effect on the amount of energy consumed. Some building materials, such as plastics, metals, glass, and certain types of insulation, require many processes, and therefore a lot of energy, to manufacture. Other building materials, such as earth, stone, timber, and concrete are more energy-efficient because they do not need so much processing before they can be used.

The materials used to construct a building will also affect how much energy is needed to heat or cool the building. One of the most effective ways to save heat energy in any building is to prevent it from escaping through the walls, ceilings, and windows. In a cool region, between 40 and 60 percent of the energy consumed in a house is usually used to heat the interior. This percentage can be reduced by

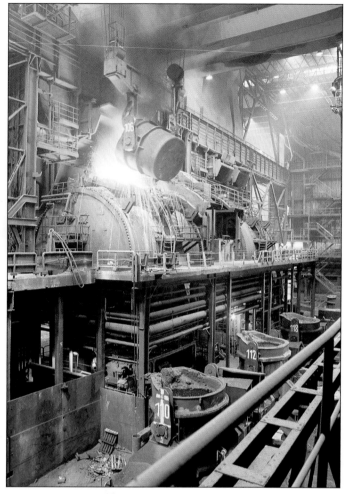

Huge amounts of energy are needed to produce steel, one of the metals often used for building.

Green building should also take into account the effect of a new building on the landscape. Traditional buildings often fit into the landscape of a particular region because they are constructed with materials from the region. However, new buildings do not necessarily have to be built from local materials to reduce their impact. In Austria, a large satellite dish sits on what looks like a green field on the side of a hill. In fact, underneath the grass lies an office network which has been carefully hidden to minimize the disturbance to the landscape. In Alabama, the new office building for a publishing company was constructed over a ravine in an area of dense woodland. The architects decided to build a bridge over the ravine rather than blocking it off, and they preserved as many of the trees as possible. In the summer the trees overhang the building and provide shade while in the winter sunlight filters through the bare branches and helps to heat the building.

Cleverly concealed. Offices lie under the hillside, in Aflenz near Vienna, Austria.

draft-proofing around windows and doors, and insulating floors, walls, and ceilings.

It is also possible to save energy at the end of the life of a building. If the materials from which the building is made are not suitable for recycling, new materials must be manufactured to take their place. Many buildings are now being converted to different uses, rather than being completely demolished and rebuilt. Even when buildings are knocked down, the materials from the old building can often be reused.

Thinking about a site
The best position for a building depends on the local climate. In cold places, a building that faces south will make the best use of the warming effects of sunlight. The building can be sheltered from cold winds by a hillside, or by trees and bushes. In hot climates, trees can be used to provide shade, and buildings can be positioned to make the most of cooling winds. All of these measures reduce the need for energy-consuming heating or air-conditioning systems.

A low-energy house in Germany, with solar panels and a conservatory.

Heat from the sun

In the future, as fossil fuels become more scarce and expensive, solar energy will be used more and more. There are two different methods of solar heating. In passive solar heating systems the sun warms a building directly through its windows. Double or triple layers of glass help to prevent the heat from escaping again. A south-facing, glass-covered balcony or a conservatory will heat up quickly and the warm air will flow through the rest of the building. On hot days, blinds can be drawn across the windows to prevent too much heat from entering the building. Passive solar heating is much more effective if the building has thick stone, concrete, brick, or earth walls and floors. These materials retain heat and help to keep the air inside the building at a comfortable temperature. Water is also good at storing heat. Some buildings have walls containing water, or water-filled columns which absorb and retain heat.

Active solar heating uses solar panels, which can be mounted on to any sun-facing surface of a building. The panels absorb the heat from the sun. The heat is stored by air or water circulating around the panels. The hot air or water can then be used to heat the building. Another type of active solar energy relies on technology developed for space travel. Satellites, space probes, and space stations all use photovoltaic cells to generate power. These cells convert sunlight directly into electrical energy. In a building, this energy can be stored in a battery and used to provide electrical power. The photovoltaic cells continue to work even in cloudy conditions, although they become less efficient.

Seeing the light

Large windows obviously ensure a lot of natural light. This is not only healthy for the people who live or work in the building, but it reduces the amount of energy needed for artificial lighting. Many buildings are now being designed with these two advantages in mind.

Artificial lighting is still necessary at night and for overcast days. The problem with conventional light bulbs is that a great deal of the energy they consume is given out as heat rather than light. It is now possible to replace these light bulbs with compact fluorescent tubes that use up to 80 percent less energy to produce the same amount of light. They can also last up to eight times longer. The E-lamp, recently developed and due to go on sale soon, is also highly energy-efficient. It has no filament but uses radio waves to produce the energy needed to make a coating on the glass glow.

Some buildings even have "intelligent" systems that sense when lights need to be turned on and off, depending on the level of natural light available.

Plants for health

Increasingly, architects are designing plants into their buildings. Scientists have shown that trees help hospital patients to recover more quickly, and that some plants absorb harmful vapors such as formaldehyde gas. NASA, the space agency, has discovered that English ivy absorbed 90 percent of the benzene in a room. Benzene is a toxic gas that is given off by some paints and glues, and is found in cigarette smoke. Plants also help to reduce the temperature of a building, by the shade that they cast and as a result of transpiration — the process by which water is given off through the leaves. In Tübingen, Germany a group of architects, botanists, and doctors worked together to design a center for medical research. As a part of the design they included a large, glazed area planted with tropical plants. The result is a light and airy building, with a healthy environment.

Saving water

Buildings in the developed world use up a lot of water, both in their construction and their maintenance. Water is an essential element in the mixing of concrete, the manufacture of many types of metal, and in the materials used for building and plastering walls. The single biggest user of water in the average house is the flush toilet — usually about 30 percent of the water consumed by a household. New designs for toilets which use far less water are already widely used in Scandinavia, and are becoming more common in other countries. These toilets use less than two gallons of water for every flush compared to five gallons for an ordinary system in the U.S.

A plan in Austria takes the principle of water conservation and recycling even further. The Gartnerhof project consists of a block of apartments and ten houses. Rainwater is collected on the roofs and used for washing and for flushing toilets. For drinking, the rainwater is filtered. An active solar system is used to provide hot water.

As the greenhouse effect increases, and temperatures rise worldwide, it is possible that maintaining a constant, unlimited water supply may become more difficult in many countries. Recycling our water may become as important as energy conservation.

The green example

The last principle of green design, but by no means the least, is that a building should be constructed with the users' needs in mind. When researchers asked the staff of an insurance company for their opinions on plans for new offices, they found that windows that open and natural light were high priorities. Another project about which employees were consulted was the new NMB Bank headquarters in Amsterdam, the Netherlands. Once again, air-conditioning was rejected in favor of opening windows. The staff of 2,000 were also involved in decisions about the materials used for the building.

The NMB Bank is an example of all the green principles discussed in this chapter. The architect, Ton Alberts, said "An office is really like you third skin. Everyone knows what your real skin is; your clothes are your second layer of skin, and the third layer is the building in which you work. And if that third skin doesn't fit, people start to feel uncomfortable in it."

The building looks unusual because of the angles of the walls — almost none of them are completely vertical. This not only reduces disturbance from the noise of the traffic on nearby roads, but it also helps to use the sun's heat more efficiently. Inside, the design of the ten units that make up the more-than-half-mile-long building ensures that no staff member has to work farther than 23 feet away from a window. Active and passive solar systems are used to generate heat and energy. Rainwater is collected and channeled to water the plants in the building. The NMB Bank headquarters is a model for the green building of the future.

A pleasant place to work. (Inset above) An aerial view of the NMB Bank headquarters, showing a series of towers linked together in an "S" shape with green spaces in between. (Main picture above.) Workers in the NMB Bank buildings can control the light and heat from the sun with blinds. Inside, sculptures, plants, and water (right) are used to make a pleasant working environment.

Looking at buildings
● How could you change your school or your home to save energy?
● Try to work out how much water you and your family use in a day. Include everything from teeth-brushing to running the washing machine. How could you cut back on the amount of water you use?

toxic – poisonous.

Temporary Shelter

Not all buildings are permanent structures. Some are put up to provide shelter for traveling exhibitions, fairs, concerts, or sports events. Other temporary structures are used to give shelter to people after disasters, when their own homes have been damaged or destroyed. Some people live permanently in temporary structures because they are nomads, moving from place to place in search of new grazing for their animals. Today, the number of nomadic people in the world is decreasing, as many choose to settle in one place, for example the Masai people of Kenya. (See page 30). However, the black tents of the Bedouin people can still be found in the deserts of the Middle East. Despite government programs to provide permanent settlements, several million people continue to lead a nomadic life in Central Asia, living in tents, called *yurts*, that are made from felt laid over a frame of willow branches.

A yurt is based on a framework of poles (inset) which are covered in felt or skins (below).

Shelter after disaster

Disasters such as earthquakes, cyclones, floods, and drought as well as wars affect many millions of people every year. Often the initial disaster sets in motion a chain of events—drought can cause crops to fail and lead to famine; flooding can mean that the water supply becomes contaminated, quickly leading to epidemics of waterborne diseases such as diarrhea and cholera. As well as medical aid and food, shelter is one of the most urgent priorities for people in a disaster area. Not only does shelter give people some protection from the weather; it also helps them to recover from the shock often experienced after a disaster. For this reason, small shelters that are suitable for families are better than large communal ones where many families are crammed in together. At least the smaller shelters give people some privacy and provide somewhere that they can call "home."

The most important points to be considered

Kurdish refugees on the border between Iraq and Turkey, using tents and makeshift shelters.

about emergency shelters are that they should be cheap, easy to transport and therefore light and compact, and they should provide adequate protection against the climate — whether hot, wet, or cold. Tents are the most common form of disaster shelters, especially tents made out of plastic sheeting. Plastic sheeting is waterproof, and black sheeting provides some protection from a hot sun. In cold conditions, tents made of thicker materials give better insulation.

Sometimes materials brought in by relief agencies or governments are used together with local resources. In India and Bangladesh, plastic sheeting has been used as a waterproof layer in between an inside and outside wall of woven bamboo to build a simple shelter. In other cases

it may be more useful to provide people with the tools to build shelter for themselves. For example, after an earthquake there may be plenty of building materials in the form of rubble and stones, but survivors may need tools and lumber to make a framework for a temporary shelter.

There have been many attempts to design emergency shelters that give more protection than tents. Dome-shaped plastic "igloos" and hexagonal plastic units were both tried out in the 1970s. However, in many cases it took

When an earthquake struck Turkey in 1975, many families lost their homes. Oxfam provided prefabricated shelters with 0.8 inch thick polyurethane walls. When stone houses had been rebuilt these temporary shelters were used for storage.

The old and the new. The tube-shaped exhibition center in Cardiff, Wales.

months for these shelters to reach the disaster area because they had to be transported complete or in large sections, which made them bulky. By the time they arrived, local people had already built some form of shelter for themselves. The cost of transporting these units was very high. Many people felt that the money would be better spent on helping the survivors of a disaster rebuild permanent houses. In many cases the shelters looked so strange that local people did not want to use them. After an earthquake in Nicaragua in the early 1970s plastic igloos were provided, but only one-third were occupied by the survivors. The rest were left standing empty.

Although there will always be a need for temporary shelter after disasters, many aid agencies and governments are now just as concerned with helping the survivors of a disaster to repair or rebuild their old houses as quickly as possible. More work is now being done with local communities to find ways that their houses could withstand a similar disaster again. (For example, see earthquake-resistant

housing in Peru, on page 30.) This approach means that some areas of the world will not need temporary shelters so frequently.

Traveling roadshows

Tents are not only used by nomadic people and for disaster shelters. Tent-like structures often provide cover for temporary exhibitions. One company has designed a structure that looks like a large circus tent. It is called The Pyramid and can seat 10,000 people for concerts and sports events. The Pyramid takes five days to erect so it will probably stay in one place for a few months rather than weeks.

Other temporary structures take different forms. A sculpture exhibition in the Netherlands was housed in a pavilion made almost entirely of panes of glass, glued together and held up by steel supports. The pavilion was dismantled when the exhibition was finished. Another moveable building used for exhibitions, in Cardiff in Wales, is a long-oval tube. It comes apart into sections which can be transported from one site to another by road. Some of the forms of shelter that are the quickest to erect are inflatable structures. These come in many shapes — domes, hangar-like shapes, and the decodome, which is a dome shape with ten arches let into the side. Air is constantly pumped into these structures to prevent them from collapsing.

Geodesic domes are often used for temporary shelter. The geodesic dome was developed by an American engineer, R. Buckminster Fuller, in the late 1940s and early 1950s. It is a globe-shaped structure made out of metal supports, often arranged in interlocking triangles. Several permanent geodesic domes have been built, including one at the Epcot Center in Florida. Perhaps the most startling proposal for a dome structure was made by Fuller in 1955 when he suggested enclosing an area of New York 2 miles wide in a giant dome to provide a completely controlled environment and protect the area from pollution.

One of the largest exhibitions of this century is being held in Spain in 1992 — Expo '92. Many of the pavilions built on an island on the Guadalquivir River in Seville are permanent structures, but some will be packed up and moved on after Expo. The Danish pavilion, for example, will be taken to Japan after Expo has finished where it will form part of a village of historic Danish buildings. Other pavilions will also be dismantled once the show is over.

Looking at buildings
- Temporary shelters for exhibitions and concerts take many forms. Try designing your own movable building. It must be easy to take apart and move, but big enough to house your event.

Inflatable structures (left) can be put up on site in minutes.
The Ski Haus (below), which houses up to four people, is carried to its temporary site by helicopter. Solar panels and a small engine provide heat.

More Houses for More People

It is estimated that over 100 million people across the world are homeless, without any form of shelter at all. Many millions more live in unhealthy and squalid conditions. The United Nations estimates that just to keep pace with the demand for shelter in the 1990s, approximately 53,000 new houses would have to be built every day.

Although homelessness is an increasing problem in the developed world, it is most serious in the poorer countries of the developing world. Each year, the number of people in the countries of the developing world rises by between 40 and 50 million — a far higher rate of increase than in the developed world. Affordable housing and access to basic services such as clean water and sewerage systems are expensive to provide. This chapter describes various projects to build more houses in different parts of the world and looks at the problems as well as the success stories.

In some parts of the world the rise in population has meant that materials traditionally used to construct shelters are becoming scarcer. In the small country of Rwanda in Central Africa houses were once built from a lumber frame, filled in with woven branches and covered with mud. As suitable lumber has become more difficult to find, it has been replaced with mud bricks. The problem is that the mud houses do not stand up well to the climate, which is often cold and damp, so people now use cement, if they can afford it, to make the houses last longer. However, cement is expensive and, until recently, had to be imported.

In some countries, building laws have prevented people from using local materials to build their houses. Kenya became an independent country in 1964, but many of the laws

Makeshift homes. Many people in developing countries have to live in slums like this one in Manila in the Philippines.

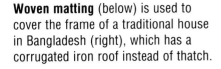

Woven matting (below) is used to cover the frame of a traditional house in Bangladesh (right), which has a corrugated iron roof instead of thatch.

established by the British remain. These include regulations that require people to build their houses out of cement, concrete blocks, and corrugated iron sheets. Roofs in urban areas have to be strong enough to withstand 6 inches of snow! Many people cannot afford these expensive materials; instead they are forced to build illegal shelters out of mud and thatch, or out of waste materials such as old cardboard. The building regulations in Kenya are now under review.

Living dangerously

Some areas of the world are prone to natural disasters, yet for many reasons people have to live in these regions. Work is now being done to try to construct buildings that are able to withstand such disasters, or that will cause as little injury as possible if they do collapse.

Floods are a frequent occurrence in Bangladesh. The country is a vast, low-lying plain through which the Ganges, Brahmaputra, and Meghna rivers run. They join to form the largest delta in the world as they flow out to sea. In 1988, floodwaters covered three-quarters of

the country, destroying or damaging 3.6 million houses and making 25 million people homeless. As well as river flooding inland, huge storm surges are swept in by cyclones from the Bay of Bengal, inundating the coastal areas. This is what happened in April 1991, when more than 300,000 people died.

For the poor people of Bangladesh, trying to build adequate shelter is a constant struggle. In the rural areas traditional houses are made from a lightweight bamboo or lumber frame with woven matting filling in the spaces. These houses have thatched roofs. They are likely to last for only two to five years, but they are relatively easy to rebuild if they are washed away, and they do not cause injury if they collapse in high winds. In places where floods are less frequent, houses are often made from mud, which has a longer lifespan. A reliable supply of bamboo for building is vital, yet there are signs that bamboo plants are not being given enough time to regrow, and that bamboo is becoming scarcer. Some research is now being done on methods of treating cut bamboo to make it last longer so that it would not have to be replaced so often.

Houses in Bangladesh could be made safer and able to withstand high winds and floods. Reinforced concrete columns could be used to strengthen the frames of houses to prevent them from collapsing. But very few families can afford such expensive measures. There are too many poor people in the country for the government or even aid agencies to be able to provide adequate funds for people in need.

The government has begun a program to construct cyclone shelters, large concrete buildings on columns, which can provide refuge for whole communities in storms and floods.

In Peru, the people of the Alto Mayo region used to build their houses with thick, earthen walls. When an earthquake hit the area in 1990, the walls disintegrated because they were not flexible enough to withstand the movement of the ground. Many people were killed or injured as buildings collapsed. A different method of building has now been introduced to the area. Together, the local community, the government, and an organization called Intermediate Technology worked out a building technique that used local materials and know-how, but which would, hopefully, stand up to any future earthquakes.

This technique, called *quincha*, involves weaving strips of reeds and bamboo in and out of a wooden frame, which is then covered with a thin layer of mud. The frame is held by a concrete foundation. This method gives the walls enough flexibility to sway, like a tree, so that in an earthquake they do not fall down. Only one year later, in April 1991, another earthquake hit the region — and the *quincha* buildings remained standing.

A concrete cyclone shelter in Bangladesh.

A changing way of life

In some regions of the world people are being forced to build new types of shelter for themselves because of a change in their way of life. In many regions more and more people are moving away from rural areas to try to find work in the large cities. Some nomadic people, who used to move from place to place with their animals, are now choosing to settle in one place. One example of this change in life-style is that of the Masai of Kenya.

In the past the Masai were cattle herders who moved from site to site every few years. Their houses, called *manyattas*, were constructed by the Masai women. They were made from a lattice-work of branches, filled with leaves and twigs, and covered with cattle dung. Each *manyatta* took about two weeks to construct and would be abandoned when the household moved on. Recently, more and more Masai have begun to settle in one place. The traditional *manyatta* is not suitable as a permanent home, so new designs and building methods are being developed.

The Masai women are now using a technique of building called "rammed earth," or *pisé de terre*. A wall is built up by filling a wooden frame with earth, which is then pounded with heavy poles. One layer of rammed earth is left to dry before another layer is added on top. When the wall is completed

A traditional Masai house (above) and a new one (below), in which the walls are made by filling a wooden frame with layers of earth (right). As each layer dries, the frame is moved up.

it can be given a protective covering of mud or lime mortar. Window openings provide light and ventilation. The rammed earth method is hard work, but it produces cheap, comfortable, and long-lasting houses.

For the many thousands of people who migrate to the world's cities every year, life is often very hard. The capital of Peru, Lima, has a population of six million. Sixty percent of these people live in squatter settlements — shelters that are illegally built with no access to vital services such as clean water or hygienic sanitation. Often, these settlements are constructed from any waste material that comes to hand — cardboard, fabric, plastic sheeting, old tires, or corrugated iron — because people cannot afford to buy building materials of any kind. The

same situation is found in all the big cities of the developing world — Mexico City, Calcutta, and Bombay, for example.

One program that aims to improve living standards for poor people in the cities of the developing world is called "sites and services." The agency running this program buys land from the government or private landowners. This land is divided into plots and sold at a cheap price to people in need of housing. In general, the plots are connected to the main water supply and to the sewerage system. People then build houses on their own plots.

The details of sites and services plans vary from country to country, and the plans have been more successful in some areas than others. In Zambia there were shortages of building

Smoky Mountain. People live and work amid the piles of rubbish dumped in a district of Manila in the Philippines. They earn money by sorting and selling some of the waste materials.

materials, such as corrugated iron roofing sheets, and because of local building regulations people were not allowed to use any other material. In Tanzania people were given only six months to build their houses. If they had not completed the houses within this time limit they would have lost their plots. For many inhabitants this was an impossible schedule because they did not have enough money to pay for the materials to build that quickly. In Malawi the program was more successful, and many people built homes for themselves and other buildings, which they rented out.

The problem with the sites and services plan is that there will never be enough plots to satisfy the demand from people needing housing. When the Dandora Project, a sites and services plan in Nairobi, Kenya, was set up, 26,000 families applied for only 6,000 plots. Another problem is that some homeless and unemployed people cannot afford even the relatively small amounts of money needed to buy a plot and build upon it. To help these people, some city authorities are working to improve the housing that already exists in the squatter settlements. This is called "upgrading."

Upgrading squatter settlements

In many places the squatters themselves have improved their housing conditions. In Mexico City the peasant families who lived in an area of squatter housing formed the Palo Alto Cooperative. When the landowner decided to sell the land on which they lived to a developer for a luxury hotel, they were able to fight their case. They eventually won the legal battle to own their land. Since then they have been able to build a clinic, community hall, chapel, dairy, and many other **amenities**, secure in the knowledge that the land is theirs.

In other cases the city authority and local squatter community have worked together to improve the conditions in squatter settlements. In the second largest city in Indonesia, Surabaja, about 40,000 people live in a squatter settlement known as a *kampung*. Between 1979 and 1982 the Kampung Improvement Program was carried out by the local authority to provide roads, sidewalks, drainage, toilets, and water pipes. Once the work was completed, the community was responsible for the upkeep of the services.

It has been estimated that between half and

Slum dwellers in Semarang in Java were rehoused and a credit program, organized by an aid agency, allowed them to borrow money to improve their new houses.

three-quarters of all the housing in cities of the developing world is built by people for themselves. Even if governments do have programs to provide housing for people, the supply cannot keep up with demand, and the houses built under such programs are often too expensive for most poor families. It seems that the way to provide more houses for people in the future is not necessarily to build for them, but to enable people to build for themselves, using local resources in the most appropriate ways.

Building-your-own-house programs

It is not only the developing world that is experiencing a shortage of housing. Many homeless people in the developed world are forced to live on the streets, in parks, under bridges, or in shelters. Many poor families are housed in public housing projects that are crime-ridden and dangerous places to live.

Given the chance, as seen in some inner-city neighborhoods, such as the South Bronx and Camden, New Jersey, low-income families can build and purchase their own homes. Unfortu-

nately, there are not enough of these programs to help everyone in need. Some of these programs are supported by the government and others are privately funded. Church groups and volunteers have been responsible for helping people provide decent housing for themselves. Former President Jimmy Carter has been seriously involved in home-building projects, such as Habitat for Humanity, and has been helping people in his own state of Georgia.

Looking at buildings

● Many families around the world have to live in just one room. What problems might they have to face in their day-to-day lives? Are there any advantages?

amenities – the facilities usually found in a town: stores, parks, a library, a clinic, and so on.

Building for Leisure and Pleasure

The Olympic Park in Munich, Germany

The shell-shaped roofs of the Sydney Opera House in Australia, the huge golfball that forms the Spaceship Earth building at Epcot in Florida, and the extraordinary tent-like roof of the Olympic Park in Munich, Germany are all examples of the strange and amazing structures that have been built for the purposes of leisure and pleasure. These buildings demand to be noticed, enticing people in to enjoy whatever attraction they have to offer—a concert or play perhaps, a sports event or exhibition.

Musical buildings

Designing a concert hall is not an easy matter. The architect has to consider not only the appearance and layout of the hall, but also the **acoustics** that will be produced when music is played in the hall. The amount of sound that is absorbed or reflected by the building and the way that the sound travels through the hall are vital questions that an architect must take into account. If the hall is too big, the sound will be soaked up by the audience when it is full. If it is the wrong shape, the sound will not reach the audience evenly.

Architects have used unusual materials to improve the quality of the sound that reaches the audience. In a hall in Toronto, woolen banners hang from the ceiling of the egg-shaped auditorium. They can be moved up and down to change the amount of reverberation. **Acrylic** panels above the platform also help to control the sound. Movable features have also been used in a new concert hall in England. The architects followed the shape of older concert halls in Europe — a long, high, box shape with the two side walls running parallel to one another. This shape helps to reflect the sound evenly. A huge wooden canopy that hangs over the platform can be raised or lowered. This helps to control the amount of reverberation in the hall. A series of fabric-covered panels along the side of the hall can also be used for this purpose. For classical concerts they are removed, but for pop concerts or conferences they are left in position to soak up some of the sound and help to make it clearer. Huge, concrete doors set high in the back wall above the platform can be opened to allow more echo for organ recitals and choral concerts.

The Symphony Hall in Birmingham, England

Strange but true

Some of the buildings constructed for leisure activities are almost too strange to be true. The world of Euro Disney, for example, takes the visitor into a kind of dreamland with fairy-tale castles, pirate ships, a Far Eastern bazaar, and even a trip to the stars. In Japan, the development of an indoor ski complex will mean that people no longer have to wait for snow on the slopes in order to enjoy a day's skiing. The complex has two 1,475-foot long ski slopes, landscaped to give the skiers the impression of a natural outdoor setting.

One of the strangest collections of buildings seen on one site is at Expo '92. Over 100 countries have built pavilions on an area of land on the island of La Cartuja in Seville, Spain. The huge exhibition will bring together new ideas from all over the world. The design of many of the pavilions reflects some aspect of life in the country that they represent.

However, some of the most futuristic structures have not been designed specifically for their interest or beauty but in order to keep visitors to Expo cool. In the summer, temperatures in Seville can reach at least 113°F. To counter the effect of the stifling heat, cooling devices at Expo include fabric sails stretched across the walkways to provide shade, groves of trees, and cooling towers which stand 100 feet high and are topped by wind catchers to funnel cool air down to the people below. Water is used as a cooling device at one

Climate control. The Aquatoll leisure center in Neckarsulm, Germany benefits from a controlled climate system.

pavilion, which has a wall of water flowing continuously down the glass at the front of the building. The power needed to pump the water back up five stories high is provided by photovoltaic solar cells (see page 21). Elsewhere on the Expo site the Palenque, a huge, white, plastic canopy that covers a theater, restaurants, and shops, is cooled by a film of water running over its surface. At the edge of the canopy a fine mist of water cools the air.

acoustics – the study of sound and the way it behaves
acrylic – a type of plastic used in paints and adhesives and to make fabric.

Keeping cool at Expo 92. The columns (left) draw cool air down to street level, and the bioclimatic sphere (above), which is computer-controlled, cools the warm air that passes over it.

Floating on Water

When space for buildings begins to run out on land, there are several alternatives: to build taller skyscrapers, to put buildings underground, or, if the site is near the sea or a lake, to build on to the water. In order to build out to sea, an artificial island is usually constructed, so although the buildings may appear to be floating on water, they are in fact securely anchored to dry land.

Building on water is not a new idea. People have lived in the marshy region between the Tigris and Euphrates rivers in Iraq, for almost 6,000 years. The Marsh Arabs still make their beautiful reed houses on small islands in the marshes or on artificial islands constructed from mud and reeds. Their way of life is now under threat from the Iraqi government, which wants the Marsh Arabs to move to new housing on dry land. On the other side of the world, high in the Andes mountains in Bolivia, the Aymara Indians also construct reed houses on reed platforms. They live on the highest lake in the world, Lake Titicaca. The most famous of all "floating" cities is Venice on the Adriatic coast of Italy. It is built on 118 islands in a lagoon, and its streets are canals. Today it is visited by over 12 million tourists every year.

Airports at sea

Two new airports in the Far East are to be built on new islands in the sea. In Hong Kong, off the south coast of mainland China, the new airport is to be at Chek Lap Kok, a tiny island close to Lantau Island. In Japan, Kansai International Airport will be constructed on an artificial island in Osaka Bay, linked to the mainland by a road and railroad bridge.

In order to create a platform big enough for Hong Kong's new airport, Chek Lap Kok will be leveled. It will then take about 94 million

A Marsh Arab house surrounded by water. The reed mats are ready for sale.

Kansai Airport (above, a model) will sit in Osaka Bay, Japan 4 miles offshore.

cubic yards of sand and rock to enlarge the island. The airport will be linked to Hong Kong Island, some 16 miles away, by a road and rail network including the world's second longest suspension bridge and a new tunnel.

The new airport terminal at Kansai in Japan will sit on its new island surrounded by a forest of newly-planted trees, specially adapted to salt water. The terminal is designed by Renzo Piano, together with his team, Building Workshop, to withstand the earthquakes that often threaten that part of the world. The advantage of having an airport out at sea, separated from the mainland, is that the noisiest part of an aircraft's approach, just before it lands, will take place over the ocean and not over other buildings. This means that the airport can work for 24 hours every day without disturbing people.

Floating worlds of the future

Many of the most spectacular projects for building on water are being proposed for Japan. These innovative ideas will help to solve the problem of lack of space on land. If they are built, it will largely be due to the highly developed engineering technology available in Japan.

One idea is to build a complete, self-contained city in Tokyo Bay. The city, called Marinepolis, would sit on a huge artificial island. To construct the island, huge concrete tubes, called caissons, would be let down into the sea and arranged in a ring on the seabed. The top of the ring would be above the surface of the water. Once the ring was in place, the seawater inside the ring would be pumped out and then replaced with earth and rubble to form a mound on which the new city would be built. This form of construction is claimed to be extremely stable during earthquakes. Marinepolis would include offices and houses as well as a transportation system, sports centers, theaters, and all the other amenities needed for a self-contained city. It would be linked to mainland Tokyo by underground roads, railways, and speed boats.

A truly floating city, called Floating Station Jonathan, would require no landfill or caisson construction because the whole structure would actually float in the water, moored by one anchor in water between 160 and 500 feet deep. A special system would be fitted to absorb the movement of the waves before they hit the city. The station would have many uses, including scientific research and leisure activities, and it would include a luxury 1,000-room hotel.

Perhaps the ultimate futuristic floating structure is the X-Seed 4000, proposed by the Taisei Corporation. This giant skyscraper is shaped like a cone, imitating the shape of Mount Fuji, a huge volcano in Japan. It would be 2.5 miles high and would provide enough living space for 700,000 people. It would generate its own electricity by using systems such as wind and solar power, and it would be designed to recycle all its waste water.

Cities for the Next Century

Cities have developed across the world as places where people both live and work, often growing up on trade routes inland, or around natural harbors. One of the biggest changes in the shape of the city has occurred in the twentieth century. In many places people have moved out to the suburbs. Residential areas in many cities have deteriorated or have been renewed, making them too expensive for the poor to afford. More and more roads have been built as the numbers of cars have increased, often cutting through once desirable areas with little thought to the effect on nearby buildings and the people in them.

Transportation systems

In an attempt to reduce car use in the city and to relieve the increasing congestion, many cities are now investing in new public transportation systems. Light rail systems run on tracks set into the road and pick up electricity from overhead wires. This kind of system is relatively cheap to install and can be laid along existing streets so that it does not require much, if any, demolition work. However, for light rail systems to be really effective in reducing the amount of traffic, they need to be planned carefully so that people can walk from their houses to the nearest stop.

Many light rail systems are being built in the U.S. and Europe. One group of architects in the U.S. has taken the idea even further and suggested that new building developments should be integrated with a light rail station. They have called these developments "pedestrian pockets." Each pocket would include a mixture of houses, stores, offices, and facilities such as libraries, clinics, and community centers. All the buildings would be laid out so that none was more than five minutes' walk from the light rail station, linking each pocket to the city center and to other pedestrian pockets. This idea is soon to be tested out in northern California.

A complete city of the future, due to be built in South Australia, will be designed around the most up-to-date transportation and communication systems. The multifunction polis (MFP) is planned for a swampy site, 9 miles northwest of Adelaide. Its aim is to incorporate the industries that will be important in the twenty-first century, such as communications and environmental management, with pleasant areas for people to live. It is designed to provide jobs and living space for about 50,000 people. The designers of the project are planning small villages surrounded by lakes and fields, connected to the high-technology industries in the area by the latest telecommunication and transportation systems. The MFP is viewed by its Australian and Japanese planners and investors as a model for the city of the future.

Green spaces

The importance of green spaces within a city has long been recognized. Central Park in New York was landscaped in the 1850s and still provides the people of New York with a green area in which to escape from city life. London is also famous for its parks, such as Hyde Park, Green Park, and Regent's Park. However, many twentieth century city developments have not responded to the need for green spaces in a city and have added green areas only as an afterthought. This attitude is now changing and many planners are introducing plants and green areas as an integral part of new projects.

In Hong Kong a new town that was planned in the 1970s includes a park at its center. The town of Sha Tin will eventually have a population of 750,000 people, packed into a small area

Shade in Shah Tin Town Park, Hong Kong, is provided in sitting and play areas.

in a valley. The cramped accommodation for the town's inhabitants makes the park an important area for recreation. It includes an open-air amphitheater, and a bandstand with a fabric roof designed to withstand the fierce typhoon winds that can reach over 150 miles an hour. There are also play areas for children designed around the theme of American and Chinese forts. A ravine, fountains, riverside walks, waterfalls, and different types of gardens all provide variety in a limited space.

In a new town in Japan the architect responsible for the layout of its center is not only planning green spaces on the ground, but also green spaces extending upward. The town of Nishiyachiyo will be a vertical garden city in which greenery is mixed with office development, a train station, a hotel, and a large department store. The architect, Emilio Ambasz, has created his "vertical garden" by constructing open metal frames, four or five blocks high. Each frame contains a flowering tree and is covered with climbing creepers. The planting

of the frames will ensure that different plants will be in flower each season. In the summer, fine mists of water will be sprayed from the frames to cool the air. And at night, lights dotted along the frames will give the whole structure a fairy-tale effect.

More "sky gardens" are found in the design for a new office building in Frankfurt by Norman Foster. The new Commerzbank building is a triangular tower. On every third floor there is a garden with trees and plants. Every office has a view of one of these green areas, and the employees of the bank have a pleasant environment in which to work.

Master planning
After the Great Fire devastated much of London in 1666, the architect Sir Christopher Wren presented the king with his master plan for rebuilding the city. He proposed siting the new buildings along straight, wide roads on a grid system. However, the king had neither the authority nor the finance to enforce such a

Plans for the Commerzbank in Frankfurt, Germany (below) show how planted areas rise up the building in a spiral. The photomontage (right) shows how the buildings will change the existing skyline.

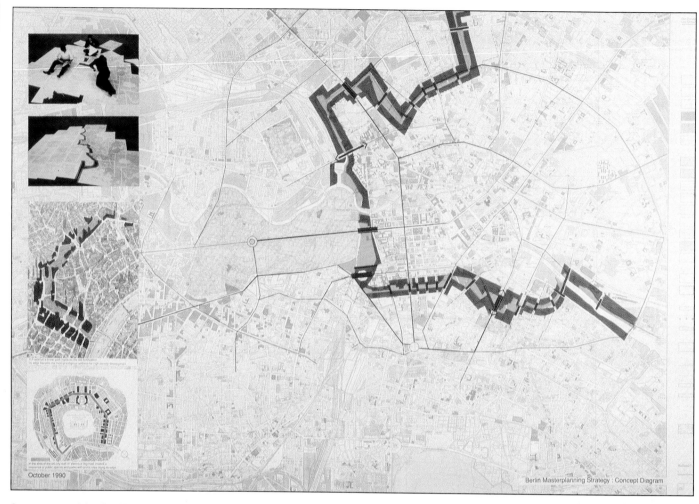

October 1990

Berlin Masterplanning Strategy : Concept Diagram

One proposal for Berlin was to construct new buildings along the line of the Wall (shown in red on the map), either side of a ribbon of open parks and gardens.

plan, and London was rebuilt haphazardly. Today, architects may be commissioned by city authorities to draw up new layouts for certain areas of the city that have become run down. This is called master planning. Several European cities, including Berlin, London, Nîmes, and Duisburg, have master plans for certain areas. In each case, the master plan covers buildings, green spaces, and transportation systems. One master plan came about when the Berlin Wall was dismantled in 1989, after it had split the city into two for 28 years. A German newspaper invited a number of architects to submit ideas of how to reunite the two halves of the city. One proposal was once more to knit together the roads that were cut by the Wall, but also to create a green ribbon across the city by turning much of the wall zone into public parks and green spaces.

In the U.S., a different approach to town planning has been taken in a new town in Florida called Seaside, on the Gulf of Mexico. The developer and architects of the town have

laid down a code that governs all the construction. It covers the type of materials that can be used, the colors that houses should be painted, and the distance between buildings. Beyond these restrictions people are free to build their own houses to their own designs.

Skyscrapers and earthscrapers
The first skyscrapers were built in Chicago and New York at the end of the nineteenth century and beginning of the twentieth. Since then almost every major city in the world has seen the construction of taller and taller buildings. In modern, overcrowded cities the skyscraper is the ideal solution to the problem of providing as much usable space on as little land as possible. Architects have experimented with some unusual shapes and designs, from the pyramid shape of the Transamerica Building in San Francisco to the glass points of the PPG Industries Building in Pittsburgh, Pennsylvania. However, some of the most innovative towers for the future are being planned for another country — Japan.

One of the main difficulties of building a high-rise tower in the overcrowded cities of Japan is the likelihood of earthquakes and strong winds. The new super-high-rise skyscrapers planned for the twenty-first century will have to be able to withstand such shocks. The proposed Taisei 100 is a 100-story, 1,575-foot tall building. It would be made up of four blocks, the bottom one octagonal in shape, the second circular, the third square, and the top block in the shape of a cross. The reason for this tapering shape is partly to make the tower more stable. The tower would also use the latest technology to ensure its safety during an earthquake, allowing the building to sway rather than collapse. An even taller tower is being planned by the Kajima Corporation. This building, too, would make use of earthquake-resistant technology. Sensors would detect any vibrations. This information would be fed to a computer which controls a system that stops the building from swaying too much in an earthquake.

The white pyramid of Transamerica Building in San Francisco.

Perhaps the most unusual of all the designs for skyscrapers for the twenty-first century is the Millennium Tower, designed by Norman Foster and the Obayashi Corporation. This super-high-rise tower is a 1,970-foot tall building topped by a 650-foot high tower — twice as high as the Sears Tower, which is the world's present record holder. It would not only include office space, but also theaters, cinemas, concert halls, shopping centers, and restaurants, provid-ing a self-contained city in the sky. It would not be built on land but 1.2 miles out on the ocean, inside an artificial lagoon protected by a sea-wall. Up to 50,000 people could live and work in the tower.

Instead of skyscrapers, some architects are in-vestigating the possibility of "earthscrapers" — whole cities built underground. In Japan this plan has the added advantage of being safer during earthquakes because the shaking effect is less below the surface than at ground level. One of these underground cities, named "Alice City" by its designers, would provide accommodation for thousands of people as well as offices, sports facilities, and other amenities, and a complete transportation network. The main problem with any deep underground building is whether

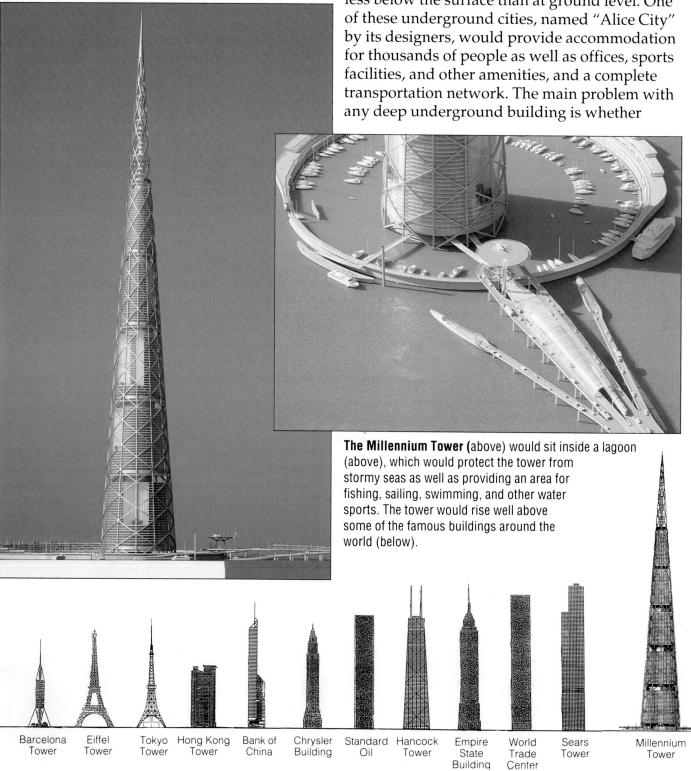

The Millennium Tower (above) would sit inside a lagoon (above), which would protect the tower from stormy seas as well as providing an area for fishing, sailing, swimming, and other water sports. The tower would rise well above some of the famous buildings around the world (below).

Barcelona Tower — Eiffel Tower — Tokyo Tower — Hong Kong Tower — Bank of China — Chrysler Building — Standard Oil — Hancock Tower — Empire State Building — World Trade Center — Sears Tower — Millennium Tower

The Biosphere II complex in Tucson, Arizona.

people will be able to cope with living away from natural daylight for any length of time.

Artificial environments

Living in space was once an idea confined to science fiction. It is now close to becoming a reality as new developments are made in space technology. One experiment in particular is likely to provide more of the information needed to set up a new settlement in space, particularly on Mars. This is the Biosphere II project, in the desert north of Tucson, Arizona. Biosphere II consists of two linked, glass-and-steel structures which are totally sealed from the outside world. One of these glass houses contains several tropical habitats in miniature — a rain forest, a small desert, even a 25-foot deep ocean with tides and a coral reef. The other glass house is used for growing food and keeping animals. Eight researchers have been living in Biosphere II since December 1990. They will live in their sealed environment for two years, growing their own food and recycling their waste products.

The aim of the experiment is partly to try to understand better how the **ecosystems** of the Earth work. But it will also help scientists to plan how the first settlers in space will support themselves, as it would be far too difficult and expensive to supply a space colony with food and fuel from Earth. It will be important for space settlers to be able to purify their air and water and grow their own food, becoming self-sufficient as quickly as possible.

The first step toward establishing human settlements in space is the American space station *Freedom*, which is due to be permanently manned in orbit around the Earth by early next century. The space station will not only be used for scientific research but also as a staging post for crews of astronauts setting out on longer space exploration flights to the moon, or to Mars.

Further into the twenty-first century, Mars is the target of an ambitious project for human settlement. It may be that, by the year 2030, humans will be living on Mars in biospheres similar to Biosphere II, carrying out the first stage of a plan to turn Mars into a new home for humankind.

Looking at buildings
- If you had the choice of living in a super-high-rise building or in an underground city, which would you choose and why?

ecosystem – the relationship between all living things on the Earth and the environment they inhabit.

43

Conclusion

In this book we have examined all types of buildings, from basic mud-and-thatch houses to high-technology skyscrapers of the future. It is clear that traditional methods of construction often provide the most suitable buildings for a particular climate and situation, despite the tendency of people in the Western world to think of these methods as primitive. Many architects are now looking once again at these methods and incorporating them into their designs. Yet there is also a place in the future for technology in buildings — to help overcome the problems of building in disaster-prone areas, for example.

There are two main challenges for the future. The first is to provide enough housing for the rapidly increasing population of the world. In Japan projects such as the Millennium Tower and "Marinepolis" are high-tech solutions to the space shortage there. In the developing countries the situation of the homeless is already acute in many cities, and drastic action needs to be taken to prevent it from becoming worse in the next century. The second challenge — energy conservation — is primarily one that faces the developed world, because it is the main energy consumer. Architects can meet this challenge through careful design, but everyone can help by energy-saving measures, such as installing insulation and using compact fluorescent light bulbs. The buildings of tomorrow are the responsibility not only of the architect designing and building them, but also the people who will live and work in them. The future is exciting, but the challenges are great.

Glossary

air-conditioning – a system of keeping the inside of a building at a constant temperature by cooling or heating air as it enters the building.
amenities – the facilities usually found in a town — stores, parks, a library, a clinic, and so on.
atrium – a large, open space, often extending several floors up in the middle of a building, usually with a glass roof to allow light to enter.
congestion – traffic jams caused by too many vehicles trying to use the same routes.
contractors – the manufacturers and builders who supply the materials and labor needed to construct a building.
developed world – a term used to describe the rich industrialized countries of Europe, North America, Japan, and Australasia.
developing world – a term to describe the poorer countries of Africa, Asia, and Latin America. Many of these underdeveloped countries have economies based on agriculture rather than industry.
duct – a tube or pipe used to carry the services of a building.

ecosystem – a unit or system in which living things interact in the environment they inhabit.
energy conservation – the principle of using as little energy as possible to make something work.
fossil fuels – coal, oil, and natural gas. They are formed out of animal and plant remains trapped in rocks.
insulation – material which does not allow heat, cold, sound, or electricity to pass through easily.
perspective – a drawing on a flat surface that gives an illusion of depth.
prefabricated – describes the manufacture of parts or the whole of a building in a factory away from the actual construction site. The parts are assembled at the site.
services – all the supplies that are needed to maintain and run a building, such as electricity, water, heating, telephone lines, computer cables, elevators, and so on.
solar energy – energy that comes from the sun.
specifications – detailed descriptions and measurements.

Index

© Evans Brothers Limited 1992
First published in 1992 by Evans Brothers Limited.